Masterplan

Also by Eric Greinke

Sand & Other Poems
Caged Angels
The Last Ballet
Iron Rose
Masterpiece Theater (with Brian Adam)
The Broken Lock - Selected Poems 1960-1975
The Drunken Boat & Other Poems From The French Of
    Arthur Rimbaud
Selected Poems 1972-2005
Up North (with Harry Smith)
Wild Strawberries
Catching The Light - 12 Haiku Sequences (with John Elsberg)
Traveling Music
The Potential Of Poetry
Beyond Our Control (with Hugh Fox)
Conversation Pieces - Selected Interviews
All This Dark - 24 Tanka Sequences (with John Elsberg)
For The Living Dead - New & Selected Poems
Zen Duende - Collaborative Poems (with Glenna Luschei)
Poets In Review
The Third Voice - Notes on the Art of Poetic Collaboration

Also by Alison Stone

They Sing at Midnight
From the Fool to the World
Borrowed Logic
Dangerous Enough
Ordinary Magic
Guzzle
Dazzle

Masterplan

Collaborative Poems

Eric Greinke & Alison Stone

PRESA PRESS
Rockford, Michigan

Acknowledgments

Many of these poems first appeared in: *Big Scream* (Grandville, MI), *First Literary Review - East* (NYC), *Forge - An Eclectic Journal of Modern Story, Culture, and Art* (NYC, Lincoln, NE, London, England), *Iconoclast* (Mohegan Lake, NY), *Lake Effect: An International Literary Journal* (Penn State University), *Plainsongs* (Hastings College), *Switchback* (University of San Francisco), *Wild Goose Poetry Review* (Charlotte, NC).

Cover painting, 2017, Alison Stone.
Photo of Eric Greinke courtesy of Anna Wylie.
Photo of Alison Stone courtesy of Michael Stone.

First Edition

Printed in the United States of America

ISBN: 978-0-9965026-8-9

Library of Congress Control Number: 2017962403

PRESA PRESS
PO Box 792   Rockford MI 49341
presapress@aol.com   www.presapress.com

Masterplan

Contents

Q & A

Tarps

Emergency

Emergency

A siren blares down the highway,
hysterically red as raw meat.
I imagine the worst disasters,
twisted bodies in crumpled cars,
stray bullets near a playground,
families trapped and screaming
or their houses on fire.
Next I think of real people,
then I hope it isn't them.

Sure, every victim is somebody's
something, but horror happening
to strangers is bearable, not
even as real as small annoyances
like running out of potato chips
during your annual Superbowl Party.
Maybe that's what it means to be
human, stuck in personal hungers,
ignoring or pretending to care
about everyone else,
one nation under fear
with justice for none.

Though we go through
the motions skillfully, and
even the siren's volume
is less than the scream of greed,
we wish for the silent strength
to somehow be more than our
natures, to match the siren's wail
with our authentic grief, to stand
alive and open in the red-tinged light.

Full Volume

The old songs still thrilled him
cranked high each morning
to serenade the potential
of another perfect day.
Outside, the meadow
crackles with pure electric
mist rising proudly
from our warm mother
while birds, though softer
than the stereo,
sing their high chorus
to celebrate dawn.
He joins in despite
the low thrum of grievances
in the wet background,
giving his voice to joy
in full-throated,
slightly off-key
explosions of brave words:
"C'mon baby, light my fire."

The Message

After Valentine's Day
the love letters began
to arrive at her hidden
cabin, so deep in woods
she thought only animals
could find the door
that she had never
locked before his
letters penetrated into
her assumed safety,
unwelcome as the bear
she'd seen ambling
in the near meadow,
there without warning
then gone the same way.
She willed him to disappear
as well, leave her peaceful,
her bare throat unmarked.
When the letters stopped
she thought that she got
what she wanted, but
felt surprisingly deflated
when the mailbox's
ivy-draped mouth
didn't praise her lips or eyes
or taunt her hardened heart,
until at last the final note
in his familiar,
jagged scrawl, which
started with her name
& ended with his,
to frame a single line:
"What lies are in a kiss."

Temptation

If only it wasn't so dark there,
& it didn't rain there every day,
& if there were no mudslides there,
& if the animals stayed in the forest,
the people might be friendlier.
Instead, everyone was edgy, waiting
for a bus, a train, a messiah,
anything to whisk them away
from a place with no air, no particular
culture, the only fashion
rubber boots & sour
looks. The only industry
was a fashionable umbrella factory.
People there bought copious cosmetics
& many personal electronic devices.
Searching for pictures of far-away,
exotic places or foamy oceans
made their fantasies of escape
their only solace in light of the
storm clouds of defeat & fear
that navigated the scary sky.
Video games with danger
& explosions calmed them
for the moment, but everything
they knew was artificial.
Time for them was numerical.
No one felt particularly special.
Even love words between
couples were delivered in
a drone
only their dogs could hear.
So that's why I declined
to purchase more property there.

The Weight

We believed we were alone, so we never saw it coming. We should have known our parents and ex-lovers were always there, waiting for the first thrill to fade. We never should have trusted our dogs and cats to keep our secrets to themselves. A clean slate's an illusion. Our flesh is cinematic and wounded cosmetically. Our hearts are kaleidoscopic and ravenous. Tabla rosa is a delusion. The only thing to do is lumber forward, clumsy with the weight. That's what puts the 'fat' in fate.

Substitution

The musical milk is flowing
down into our mouths. Why pay
when you can get it free? Why
shell out a hundred bucks
for some fame-bloated rocker
when every park has
a bandstand, and there are
herds of wannabes happy
to give it away? We drink
weak skim milk
and call it cream,
watch reruns when we dream.

Wanderlust

Spring's first warm day slapped him into action. Wanderlust hit him hard, like a sudden itch too deep to scratch. Wild with confinement, he unfolded and refolded maps, shoved nuts and a compass into vest pockets, left the breakfast dishes crusting in the sink. He was halfway up the hiking trail before he remembered that he hadn't locked the door. Should he trust the luck white bell-shaped flowers tolled? Upon consideration, he decided to place his trust in the 200 lb. orangutan he'd left guarding 'the fort.' The beast could just as easily share his fruit and wardrobe with intruders as fight them off, but sometimes looks are enough. Orange flashed before his eyes in the form of a Baltimore Oriole singing a sweet song of spring. Swaying to the beat, he raised his primate arms. A passing policeman thought the gesture odd, because he hadn't even placed The Subject under arrest, yet. Oblivious to the seriousness of his badge, The Subject answered his initial question with the knock knock punch line, "Orange you glad I didn't say banana again." He was down on the range, thinking of an orange Grange Hall, when he heard the explosion. He turned to see an orange ball of fire fill the sky. As it flew toward him like a meteor, he was overwhelmed again with feelings of wanderlust.

Stage Craft

Was it ego, she wondered,
as she felt herself swelling with
their praise, or was it something deeper
that had eluded her
for her whole life, something
meant to be, cosmic or
karmic? She couldn't decide.
But when they turned their attention
toward her sister, she wondered if
the way to draw them back
would be to feign a faint or tell
the joke about the snake and the nun.

Landlocked

The old photo album was the only place
his mother and his ex-wife smiled near each other,
just as the tree fort of his childhood was the only
place where he and his brother never fought.
On a windy day, rocking in their fort,
they had really been the best of friends,
but back on the solid, stable ground,
away from the influence of the breeze,
their filial love fell inexorably down.
If only he and his ex had had such a place,
bright with fresh air and affection, far above the jabs
and disappointments of their heavy lives.

Another Highway

We arrive at the depot
with empty pockets & loose
handcuffs, unwilling to
spend another Saturday
with sex & television,
knowing even watching buses
depart & arrive will
impart the illusion of
a metamorphosis toward
open roads & hearts,
the engine's rumbly
voice an admonition
to avoid stagnation,
to keep our motors
running in neutral.
Isn't a bus a kind
of prayer, a yearning
sent out over hills
in anticipation of
a major achievement
won by movement alone?
If the answer's No,
at least our souls
opened in asking
the question, newborn in an old
vehicle, burning up the road
fueled by high test hope.
And if it's Maybe,
we'll keep moving, headlights
slicing the dark
ribbons, wheels eating
up the road, destination
unknown. We are fueled by
dreams of highways leading

to surmountable danger,
leaving us with stories
to inspire many pop songs,
travelogues & epic novels.
We get a feeling for leaving.
For packing light.
For showing up
rumpled & ready
for action or rage
to propel or chase us
with powerful wings.
And does it matter
really if we drive
or are driven, as long
as we see mirages,
follow floating lights
& never truly arrive?
Does it matter if
the road ends
at another
foolish fork,
another deal
with an unknown devil?
Our hearts are traded
for more rambling days
before the handcuffs tighten.

Bad Actor

The gunman surprised us
when he leapt out on stage.
His eyes were cold as he took aim
at the man in the front
row loudly unwrapping
caramels, instead of at the actor
pretending to menace
the tied-up mayor and his wife.
The other actors froze
and the audience thought it
part of the show, even after
the real blood began to flow.

Solved

After the raven on the lawn
and the pasta squiggled to hieroglyphics
in the bowl, it was no surprise
when the basement door flew open
and there you were, conspicuously revealing
the last clue, that skeleton key.
If only one of us remembered
where we hid the locked box.
We walked 500 paces into the past
and tried to remember
who we were then
and what we would have done.
My striped leggings and
practiced half-smile
should offer a clue, but
we were in a different mood.
It was a key that used to open
everything in a house. But now,
a combination was needed,
something about forgiveness
and deft fingers, three turns
to the left to clear the lock,
and a satisfying click to climax.
I'm so pleased you dropped that key.

Without Wolves

A small girl with big eyes
wandered into a woods, her
errant ball a mere
excuse for following
her own desire. She
threw the ball again and
again, farther each time,
drawn by the odd chorus
of birdsong mixed with
the hollow hammering of an axe.
Leaves crunched beneath
her sneakers as she
tripped into the clearing.
When the chopper saw her, he
paused and smiled, showing
bright pointy teeth.
She happily bared her own
fangs and ran toward him with
the recognition children haven't
learned to question yet.

Occupied

Another morning, the children
squawking like gulls at the
table, a stray deer
in the backyard,
listening to the wind.
Another chance to take
or turn away from,
another wild, weedy
space to enter or
burn, to be us or them.
A spontaneous cease-fire
presents a neutral moment.
If only the Middle East
were this easy, half-chewed
food stirring paroxysms of laughter
so much better than slaughter.
If only our little ears
only heard warn
of impending explosions.
How to joy, never
had to strain to make peace in this
torrid world, when
humor eludes us
like disappearing ink?
How to gather our wits
and families, shelter inside
moments bright as the deer's
ever-watchful eyes?
Nothing to choose between
running with the herd or
striking out toward
individual danger. It
all leads to

a dead-end canyon,
when what we really want
is to fly away like cool gulls.
The splotched sky's turquoise
blends to blue-gray – no
defended borders, no manifesto
but the manifesto of light
rinsing the neutral sky, with
us one solar flare from gone.

Default

After the fire at the firehouse,
the firemen were banned
from lighting recreational bonfires.
The hunting club outlawed
dogs after the president's Lab
shot him – the loaded gun
on the truck's seat, the eager puppy
leaping. The school superintendent
called an emergency meeting to ban
band instruments after the incident
with the tuba and on the strong
recommendation of the proctologist.

The Chain

Inside the pavilion, coyotes eat
the remains of another birthday
celebration: chicken bones, chocolate cake,
grease-soaked napkins printed
with balloons. Their devouring
another sort of ritual – hunger
immediate as death at the front door.
Vultures wade through roadkill
like happy diners at a cheap buffet.
For now the balance holds –
each group satisfied, conflict
limited to brief skirmishes
at the garbage can or
furtive movements glanced
from a safe distance.
The birthday child dreams
of clowns, smiles wide
as the coyotes' toothy
grin. The sun smiles
overhead, a festive mirage,
while the vultures fly off to
sustenance and celebrations
repeating like the circles vultures'
wings slice through the blue.

After The Freeze

Crocuses poking up beside
six foot snow mounds
seem like old friends
who call after years of
cold shouldering, anger now
forgotten as the easy banter
resumes like buds
bursting from old branches
unclenching like fists.
When the snow melts
long-frozen odors leak
from the bleeding earth,
what was hidden
now emerging to
pollinate memories
both hot & cold,
until what blossoms
shines with
the familiar false hope
of fresh flowers.

Little Novels

1. Blown

After you let the dog out
he whimpered at the base of the
lightning-scorched pine.
A lone crow, it's caw the sound
of a loud drone, fluttered down.

2. Harvest

Leaning against the old barn
was your splintered axe handle.
The dead roses were scattered
on the ground like summer dreams,
indecipherable, shrivelled hieroglyphs.

3. Preparations

Field mice are migrating to warm basements,
leaving droppings behind boilers, plumping up
on stashes of candy. Even the pets
are thickening, their new fur
their only preparations for the coming winter.

4. Turning

Surrounded by fall's brightest leaves
an old wooden rowboat rots
beneath a newly naked oak.
Tubers float freely on the lake,
their shadows mottle the circling fish.

5. Doppelganger

The day the mirror fought back was weird.
The kettle whistled battle hymns
and the Pekingese wolf-howled.
Oddest of all was the framed glass,
bulging with the reflection of my enemy.

6. Artifact

The poodle was the first to notice
the plastic amulet in the cereal box.
The old man felt the sudden drop
in atmospheric pressure in his left
ventricle, a command to return the treasure.

7. Life Mimics Art

Inside their imaginary castles, dreamers
only wake when dragon's breath
cracks wish-curtained windows and
they're hurtled back into the world of
artificial illuminations and expectations.

8. Digital Age

Needing escape from the orange
evening sky, they stare too long
into various stupid screens,
gone insipid, color-blind and
choosing this torpor over rapture or oblivion.

9. Sinking Fast

When all the icebergs are gone,
and the polar bears have lumbered
into extinction, and the sea has swallowed
the coast, from our submerged cities
to the mountains, will hope float?

10. Off Key

The out of tune guitar leaning
in the corner was a special
gift to a supposed best friend,
who left it exposed and unused.
Mice nest in it, leave droppings.

11. Crisis

In the Third World, bartenders and hairdressers
serve beauty and forgetfulness to dreamers
while empty stomachs twist and bright
boots echo amid whispers of another coup or
the availability of the latest cell phone.

12. Heavenly

After the giddy astronomers
celebrated their discovery of
water crystals on one of Saturn's moons,
the fundamentalists recoiled in horror.
Luckily, another shooting wiped this off the news.

13. Legends Of The Fall

The wind whispered across the treetops,
proverbs of winter that fat squirrels
understand. Steadily they gathered, while the last
stubborn clusters of leaves hung on and
added their sighs and rumors to the song.

14. Dry Enough

Western wildfires burn out of control, a
greater conflagration than predicted, proof that
anything made dry enough can burn. News crews
and do-gooders rush to the scene, while
wealthy athletes pay fines to water their lawns.

15. It's A Wrap

Turned into a movie set, the street
morphed into what it wasn't.
Some houses transformed into candy,
while others became tombs or churches.
The star's beagle peed on the fantasy.

16. Spin Doctor

Her many plates spun on wands of
fantasy, such fervent wishing almost
a religion, her costume jewelry twinkling
in desire's spotlight. The audience gasped
as she confidently removed the wands.

17. Divine Intervention

After the dog ate the only copy of my thesis,
I considered trading him at the shelter
for a gecko, then wrote a better paper
on how truth hides behind cliche. The dog
accepted my apology, as Co-Author.

18. New Blue

Trying to find balance between the soft
underbelly of a shark and its teeth,
I reminded myself to take a break
from recreational skin-diving, then I
traded wetsuit for satin dress. Danced hard.

19. Infinite Fun

In an ironic twist of fate, the parrot
landed on the bird watcher's
head, the cat chased the boxer under
the bed, and the neighbors' piebald pony
climbed a dead oak tree like a monkey.

20. White Washed

After spring-warm weeks, the sudden snow
snaps us into winter, without nostalgia.
After two days of high wind and sleet,
our bodies magnetize to the South,
we eat like bears, rest under our flowered quilt.

21. Another Dimension

In the larger context, how could we know
if the butterfly not fluttering in Maine,
failing to bring the storm that would have
toppled the Asian dictator, was a good thing
or something weird, in another dimension.

22. Look Up in the Sky

When the dog ate raisins and lived, we knew
he was probably a Superdog, so we fed
him some onions and dark chocolate,
and he survived, indicating a
humble mutt can be God in disguise.

23. Way Down Below

At the bottom of the ocean, my
childhood tire swing sways
as fish dart through it toward
used condoms and half-eaten
memories of a sunken childhood.

24. Unscripted

The scent of strawberries reminded him
of his first love, and the time he took her
to see Ingmar Bergman's Wild Strawberries,
shown in the campus theater. They were
incompatible, he realized, when she dozed.

25. Sucker Punch

We should have let it go, but instead
we dressed it up in taffeta and spangled tights,
paraded it in front of friends who soon
wished to be elsewhere. We never
even saw us coming.

26. Feline Intervention

Unsure if the hissing cat
was sincere, the stupid man
put his hand out and got
a deep puncture wound, but
found true love in the E.R.

27. Barter System

Frequent moves left Lola indebted to the
pals who kept loading and unloading
her boxes, paid only in pizza and beer,
the kind of friend she might become
if she was more into carbohydrates.

28. Called Back

The college reunion invitation made him
wince, as he remembered
the last one, and the enormous
blunder he'd committed when he
called his wife the class slut's name.

29. The Beaten

The sad marching band ran from the field, their
plumed hats drooping, out-of-tune instruments
held to their chests. They'd practiced for weeks
but their routine had been derailed by
serial love affairs in the rhythm section.

30. Not On Display

The box of old photographs
gathered dust on a shelf
in the cluttered closet
of an unused guest room.
Kept the past safely contained.

31. Time Warp

Anomalies in the space-time continuum indicate
that too much WiFi has disrupted
the electronic frequencies of the galaxies,
causing individuals to meet their past and future
with the wrong stars in their eyes.

Q & A

1. Noise

What kind of fool am I?
The kind with stars for buttons, seas behind your eyes.

Are the oceans tired?
No, they're just distracted.

What is your real name?
I've looked, but I can't find it.

Where can I find love?
In dreams.

What have you lost?
Nothing.

What hides in your heart?
Ghosts.

What does your silence hide?
The noise of the universe.

Where are you going?
I'm going to sleep.

2. Animals

What don't dogs tell us?
That we don't deserve them.

What do cats dream about?
The kill.

What does the ostrich see in the sand?
Darkness spotted with the bodies of rocks.

Do worms know enough to fear birds?
If they see one, they try to escape.

Do quails have fun?
Yes, when football takes the place of hunting.

Do mice know joy?
When the cat's away.

Where do the bears go while they slumber?
Into peaceful caves.

Why do humans think they're smarter than dogs?
They mistake opposable thumbs for wisdom.

3. The Price

What is the worst law?
The Law of Gravity.

What are the side-effects of humility?
An open mind and inability to vanquish.

How much is a life worth?
More than the living know.

Why are snowflakes unique?
There is one for every soul.

What is the opposite of gray?
A rainbow climax.

What's the funniest thing of all?
The riddles toddlers tell.

What is the saddest thing?
Regret for one's own past.

What is better than wit?
Witness.

4. Holy Crap

What do angels wear?
All the colors we can't see.

What kind of shoes do angels wear?
Silk, spun with miracles.

What do they eat?
Dreams of peace.

Where do they live?
On heads of pins.

Who can see them?
Anyone with a heart.

How can you spot an angel?
The label on the cage.

Is love of money the root of all evil?
No, it's just one of the branches.

Is the spirit different than the soul?
Yes, the soul has a better rhythm section.

5. Monkey Time

What time is it?
Time for regret to give way to desire.

Where are the hidden colors?
Behind the lost chord.

Why is the sky blue?
It lost its one true love.

When is it time to quit?
When time runs out.

What is the price of freedom?
Blood and honesty.

Why get up?
Sunlight, stiff muscles, and hope.

What does the moon seek?
The water of our bodies.

What time is it now?
The time desire fades to habit or regret.

6. Heavy Metal Mysteries

Why did Wendy O. Williams kill herself?
She could no longer see the angels.

Why did Marianne Faithful record with Metallica?
To make them cool for Lou Reed.

Why didn't Aerosmith break up?
All they have is each other.

Why did Lou Reed record his final album with Metallica?
Metal is punk's half-sister.

Why did Metallica perform with Lady Gaga?
They were hungry and hoped she'd wear a meat dress.

What is your favorite album?
Bringing It All Back Home by Bob Dylan.

Why was Metallica inducted into the Rock & Roll Hall of
Fame?
To keep Black Sabbath company.

Who is the most shocking rocker?
The late, great Wendy O. Williams.

Tarps

Tarps

Sometimes, when a siren sounds,
or when a swimmer is out too far,
the tenuousness of our bodies
smacks us in the face like a wave
of electroshock sympathy.
Brutal reports from abroad
stoke the fear we try to
soothe with beer and
quasi-patriotic tears,
but we really weep for ourselves.
Aren't we all soldiers
armed with heavy
weapons and defended
by rigid body armor?
Aren't we all fighting for reasons
we don't fully understand,
like too many rats
jammed into a cage?
Sometimes death's gleaming
grin makes us tender
as water, while other
times we turn to ice.
Rare flashes of good news –
reunited siblings, a stray
dog that miraculously
intuits its way home –
slice grief's turbid sky. Our
faces, for the moment, shine.

Fanfare

The outpouring of love
for the dead rock star
made him wonder
if he'd missed something.
He'd never cared
for *that* kind of music.
He was more into jazz,
and he'd didn't like
the dead man's hairstyles.
Not wanting to be left out
he bought the Greatest Hits,
willed himself to find the thrill.

The Arrow

A thing with feathers flies
by my open bedroom window.
A pillow, punctured and oozing,
flung by the screaming
meanies in my neighborhood,
explodes into a hopeless cloud.
Nothing to make a wish on,
like a dandelion's blown fuzz
or a stone tossed into a deep well.
Then a loud chirping sound erupts from
the street – bird or drunk teenager?
Perhaps a ringtone, signaling
a call that would save me
from the bed I made myself?
Or an admonition, something
forgotten or ignored
buzzing in my skull?
But no, it really is a bird,
drab-feathered and small,
winging skyward as
fast as lost dust.
I am wishing myself up,
gliding with the bird toward
oaks' raised arms, or at least
to the top of the cedar fence.
I like the view, but still don't know where
to find a landscape or a song
to fill me up and never stop.

String Theory

She wandered through
the canyon streets
in search of an open
throat, a song to
tie her yearnings
to. Tired of her story,
she wanted a melody
to transport her far away
to a place where everything
shone in the present
tense, unmuddied by her
needs and preconceptions
but instead fast flowing
to a peaceful pool where
her heart felt clean
as the bright fish,
silver flickers
in the shallow water
that dissipate to a
weightless universe.
She couldn't recall where
she'd felt this before –
childhood sandbox afternoons,
perhaps, or hours
spent flying through light
on the old tire-swing
buoyed up by a living bough,
her stomach lurching
joyfully with each descent,
her body part of the sky.
She came back down
when an unexpected shadow
emerged from a doorway
asking the time –

an innocent, banal
request that trapped her
momentarily in between
the past and present before
she realized whose voice
introduced her to prim, British
vowels – her old seamstress.
Tiny stitches, indestructible knots.

Passing Through

Here in this ghost town,
more like Pompeii than Texas,
it's as if they all walked off to
museums to be examined and
cataloged – woman in faded print dress,
man whose shoulders slope with
the shape of outcast hours.
Here at the city limits of hope,
transfixed by tumbleweeds rolling
as though they, too, were seeking
exit or escape from this soul-numbing,
barren land, the endless dust.

Man Cave

Thick summer air pressed him
down onto the den couch. Despite
wheezing breezes expelled from
an ancient air conditioner, he
couldn't get comfortable, the heat
intractable as his ex-wife
on politics, religions & how
to cook & eat spaghetti.

Her smug twirling of oiled
al dente strands always
reminded him of seaweed
swirling in shallow water.
Why had he floundered so long
beneath her brine-green gaze?
Why hadn't he floated away
like a loose balloon?
He always had trouble exiting,
however unpleasant his
nausea, however heavy
the dooming humidity.

Why believe there was a better
elsewhere where his body
would cooperate? Why
not a surrender to the grand
scheme of inertia, the limp
acceptance of days, years
spent sleeping? After all, fat
Teddy Bears make the best pillows.

Accusation

After her long walk to
an unknown destination,
the escaped prisoner was
anxious to ditch her
tell-tale orange jumpsuit
and explore the
freedom she'd only
dreamt of just hours
before the walls fell.
What to do first? Devour
the edgeless sky or follow
signs to the Museum of
Human Hamburger? She wanted
to leap skyward, but that would
attract unwanted attention before
she was sure how
the locals would greet her.
Would they understand
her special kind of
sign language? Would
they overlook her bulbous
nose, smacked by a
falling wall as she ran?
Would the scratches
of the now dead watchcat
be like a speaker that blared
out a savage alarm? Why had
she stolen the wheelbarrows
anyway? And why did she
confess? Why not
plead the Fifth? The
truth hurt, but what
about the dirt piles that
she'd used to hide

evidence? Didn't obfuscation
cause a deeper ache?

Petals And Roots

The storm shifted slightly, pummeling
the neighboring village. That and a fortune cookie
implied that we were having good luck,
that our feng shui was impeccable, our bearing regal.
So why did the begonias droop and an odd
foreboding hang over the table?
Were they aware of something that we weren't?
Was it karma, fate or luck?
Perhaps some past misdeeds crawling
up from guilt's sewer, or
maybe they were victims of over-watering.
Maybe tomorrow another storm will come, to
test the gods' good will, confirming our favor
or hammering us with the icy bite of
a Plutonian spasm. Snow storms in
the Milky Way head our way, evidence
of cosmic inattention to our desires,
or perhaps a test of fortitude. Too easy
for the colors of the heavens
to reflect the dark human soul.
Too hard to cling to calmness as precipitation
batters the roof, our equanimity fickle
as an Arizonian monsoon, flooding the
desert with unexpected flotsam and jetsam.
Too human to greet fortune's turns with
clenched teeth and the opposite of prayer.
Wild lilies smile in sunlight.
By night they dream of running.
The thick sky covers them in
all luck's colors, blended
into shifting spectrums for our hungry eyes.
They may know something that we don't,
may know how to ride fortune's crests
with their petals open, roots intact.

Fall

Walking near a row of
halfway-to-red maples, he realized
summer was nearly gone.
She had made it the best summer ever.
He flushed redder than the leaves
remembering her intricate
stories about her childhood,
and how they drew him in like a
hungry orphan smelling
pancakes browning in someone
else's kitchen. Her eucalyptus lotion
evoked the image of his grandmother.
Her hair scrunchies called back his
swimming coach. Nostalgia followed her
through fields of excitement,
like bees on the scent of
almost forgotten sweetness.
He was never just himself
when he was with her, instead
he grew into a giant, ready
to conquer his own awkwardness
and save them both from
being battered by the flying debris
of another unrequited connection.
All his lonely past selves snuggled
next to her on the couch,
waiting for the dead leaves
while he walked weakly away.

The End?

The double rainbow was the first sign,
followed by the owl with a misshapen
wing. When the river turned
to blood, the Vampire Bats
became badly bloated,
and the local blood bank
started systematically siphoning
from the abandoned boat launch.
Then the Silver Maples tarnished.
Every mom-to-be gave birth
to twins. The dogs meowed.
Atheists learned prayers, just in case.

On Call

The problem with old friends
was that they always resurfaced
on sunny mornings when his craving
for a human connection
temporarily blinded him
to their mercurial shadows.
He always dove back in,
opening too much, surprised
when they showed
the same old callous regard,
same shallow values, yet
mysteriously appealing smile.
How long could he overlook
their droning about ex-wives
and hot conquests, their need
for a magic mirror
to reflect their brilliance
and royal entitlement?
How had he ended up back
in a supporting role, murmuring
"Rhubarb, rhubarb" while
wolves disguised as sheep
eyed him as potential prey?
Where did he lose the old
grudge-holding, self protective
self that saw through
pretty wool and witty repartee?
Though tortured by doubt,
he snatched up the phone.
"Good to hear from you." he said.

The Gate

Words above the gate admonished us
to abandon all hope if we entered,
but we'd traveled too far to turn back.
We'd left the disappointments
and punishments of daily life,
journeyed to this new
plateau propelled by faith alone.
What we thought was perpetual light
reflected backward into shadow,
tempting us onward, our steps
quickening, our pockets
heavy with coins and
unfulfilled dreams. What we thought
was an endless summer soon dimmed
into this darklight, chillbone winter.
We shivered and plowed on,
the shadows swelling, our breaths
billowing like shades of
white silk, turned pink by the sunset.
Our footfalls echoed off cold
walls and ceilings of concrete.
Where was the knowledge
we'd come for? Past
crimes and failures
summarized into a moral imperative?
Where did we begin and me end?
A blast of heat roared from the door,
shocking my numb skin. Maybe that's
the answer – how easily the frozen air is
sliced by fire, just as we
enter the realm of our dreams.
We crashed down on solid ground,
hearts fueled by sounds
of the night sky and its beautiful

inhabitants. We let go of questioning
and looked up at the stars.

Done

Six feet deep and still falling,
the obstinate snow
piled waist high to windowsills
denies possibilities of crocuses,
their bright splashes
foreign and impossible
in this white glare,
neutralizing everything in
one long note,
a gentle, absolute erasure.

In The Dark

Sorry that Pluto is no longer a planet. Sorry that Tower
Records closed. Sorry that Manhattan's pushcarts
transmogrified into sad telephones. Regrettable that
deer munch manicured suburban lawns, their busy teeth
chomping Kentucky Bluegrass. Unfortunate that
clouds closed the moon's wide eye. A shame that
no one seems to feel responsible for the waste of
tears spilled for unworthy lovers, or the extra
miles traveled by rejected immigrants running for their
    lives.
Easier to focus on how regrettable it is
that the cost of living rises, than on the tragic
spaces between family members, pulsing with
traumatic long-term tensions and unresolved trust.
Sorry, also, that the Pinta Island Tortoise and Chinese
    Paddlefish
swam into oblivion, and isn't it sad how the poor are
paddling in place, their resignation a different kind of
whirlpool, swirling inexorably into itself? Almost
    criminal that
pollution causes 1 in 7 deaths, our waste and poison
bombarding both personal and global immune systems.
Sad but no surprise that things so often break down, the
    excess
of some robbing others of bare necessities, with no real
opportunity for change, though the few, golden exceptions
go viral on the internet, neutralizing our consciences.
Regrettable, too, how technology fills our bedrooms with
anti-erotic red LED numbers and TV screens screaming
crime and war and the occasional hard-luck adoptable dog.
In the larger scheme, perhaps it's better that we don't
look too hard, but rather, turn our guilty eyes
toward the invisible dark matter that keeps the cosmos
    whole.

Chaos Theory

While we were gone, something happened to
the furniture. The table tipped alarmingly, the blue
chairs entangled in an orgy on the patio, our new
palm tree an uprooted voyeur. How
did your laptop end up in the refrigerator? Why
the stereo wire coiled tight around
the neck of your mannikin? Were we somehow
the cause of the chaos, our disturbed
projections going poltergeist? Or was it
the larger world's upheavals, brought into
too much perspective? Could we
tidy everything back up into denial
of our own complicity, or was it too late?
We couldn't unsee the smashed
viola stuffed into the dirty-clothes hamper, or
scrub the smirk from the carpet. Still, there
was the thrilling release of sudden loss, the
possibilities made visible by
an invisible wave that rearranged our priorities.
Made space in the new arrangement for
the new nebulae that we bought today, for
new swirls of color and new ways to praise
our suspense in the quiet after the storm.

Peanuts

Turning and turning in the wind,
the tree-trapped kite
forever taunts poor Charlie Brown. Lucy
holds the football faithlessly, while he
puts everything he has into his slapstick
kick. I always wanted to be Snoopy,
but I would have settled
for Woodstock. At least he
can fly off when things get
predictable, and doesn't
Linus really get it best,
waiting for the Great Pumpkin?
That faith is more important
than candy, and anything
great is worth waiting for.
No one can eat just one.

Night Of The Damned

Graveyards are sprouting up already.
One neighbor has a ghost
in the hedge, a large stuffed spider
with springy orange legs
hangs in mock menace
from their lamppost, and two
skeletons pose among the
final hardy roses. The blow-up
witch, swaying in the wind, offers
a cartoon version of the real
thing, meant to convert fear
to fun, but instead she makes a
point about power, how victors
write the history books, converting
healers and midwifes to warty-nosed
cannibal kidnappers. Paper mache
monsters with glued-on features
distract us from the fiendish
killers in suits trying to soothe us
with rhetoric on TV, and fool us
into thinking fear's a choice.
At night some of the ghosts
look real, and we take pains
to avoid the local cemetery, in case
campfire stories get their terror
from something more than
our imaginations, and the shadows
in our childhood memories
have a death of their own.
On Halloween, all the children are
touched by phantoms, the ones who
reach bloody rubber fingers to grab
for candy, and the timid ones who hide
behind ferocious make-up,

daring to hope for kindness
from random strangers.
Masks and pageantry reveal our
world's true face – monsters mingling with heroes,
so much hidden, haunting, sweet.
We hide in our sincere patches
awaiting the arrival of the Great Pumpkin,
tempting fate with faith.

Final Heat

Summer's last stand – the air
thickens. Children laugh and whine
in wading pools, dogs seek
friendly faces, their sweet
eyes shining with higher love.
Vegetable stands line the highways,
hand-lettered signs
promising freshness, hoping
to lure drivers on their way
to or from Home Sweet Home.
Thoughts of new school clothes
infect the suburban zeitgeist, while
parents cross rulers and crayons
off lists, shave pencils sharp
as the mean girls' smiles.
As the first accomplished maple leaves
enter their red retirement, burning
brilliantly right before extinction,
the other trees ready themselves,
the animals' fur thickens
imperceptibly. There's still time
for a few leaps into a lake,
or one last trip to a dusty
amusement park before the
water's chill evicts us
and the wooden
horses clip-clop away.
Long-gone stars glow here
and now, light years away
from an unknown tomorrow.

Eric Greinke has an M.S.W. from Grand Valley State University. His poems and essays have been published internationally in hundreds of literary journals, such as *Abraxas, California Quarterly, Delaware Poetry Review, Forge, Gargoyle, The Green Door* (Belgium), *Ginyu* (Japan), *The Journal* (U.K.), *Main Street Rag, New York Quarterly, Paterson Literary Review, The Pedestal Magazine, Poem, Prosopisia* (India), *Schuylkill Valley Journal, South Carolina Review,* and *University of Tampa Review.* His most recent book is *The Third Voice - Notes on the Art of Poetic Collaboration* (Presa Press, 2017). His website is: www.ericgreinke.com

Alison Stone has an M.F.A. from Pine Manor College. Her poems have been published in many literary journals, such as *Barrow Street, Chelsea, The Illinois Review, Michigan Quarterly Review, The New Statesman, The Paris Review, Ploughshares, Poet Lore, Poetry,* and *Poetry International.* Her first book, *They Sing at Midnight,* won the 2003 Many Mountains Moving Poetry Award. Stone is also the recipient of *Poetry's* Frederick Bock Prize and *New York Quarterly's* Madeline Sadin Award. Her most recent books are *Guzzle* (Dancing Girl Press, 2017) and *Dazzle* (NYQ Books, 2018). Her website is stonepoetry.org

Catalog

John Amen
At The Threshold Of Alchemy
ISBN: 978-0-9800081-5-9; 86 pgs.; $13.95.
Guy Beining
Nozzle 1-36
Chapbook; 40 pgs.; $6.00.
Louis E. Bourgeois
Alice
Chapbook; 40 pgs.; $6.00.
Alan Catlin
Walking Among Tombstones in the Fog
ISBN: 978-0-9965026-4-1; 72 pgs.; $13.95.
David Chorlton
Bird on a Wire
ISBN: 978-0-9965026-5-8; 64 pgs.; $13.95.
Joan Colby
Her Heartsongs
ISBN: 978-0-9965026-7-2; 76 pgs.; $13.95.
Kirby Congdon
Selected Poems & Prose Poems
ISBN: 978-0-9772524-0-4; 84 pgs.; $15.00.
Athletes*
ISBN: 978-0-9831251-0-5; 52 pgs.; $9.95.
Remarks And Reflections - Essays
ISBN: 978-0-9888279-5-0; 96 pgs.; $17.95.
*Kirby Congdon: 65 Years Of Poetry - A
Bibliography of His Poems, Prose Poems and Criticism*
ISBN: 978-0-9888279-0-5; 132 pgs.; $20.00
Hugh Fox
Blood Cocoon - Selected Poems Of Connie Fox
ISBN: 978-0-9740868-9-7; 72 pgs.; $15.00.
Time & Other Poems
Chapbook; 44 pgs.; $6.00.
Eric Greinke
*The Drunken Boat & Other Poems From The French Of
Arthur Rimbaud*
ISBN: 978-0-9772524-7-3; 108 pgs.; $15.95.

The Potential Of Poetry - Essays
ISBN: 978-0-9831251-1-2; 88 pgs.; $11.95.
Conversation Pieces - Selected Interviews
ISBN: 978-0-9831251-6-7; 100 pgs.; $15.95.
For The Living Dead - New & Selected Poems
ISBN: 978-0-9888279-2-9; 160 pgs.; $15.95.
Poets In Review
ISBN: 978-0-9965026-0-3; 124 pgs.; $15.95.
Zen Duende - Collaborative Poems (w/ Glenna Luschei)
ISBN: 978-0-9965026-1-0; 64 pgs.; $13.95.
The Third Voice - Notes on the Art of Poetic Collaboration
ISBN: 978-0-9965026-6-5; 84 pgs.; $13.95.

Ruth Moon Kempher
Retrievals
ISBN: 978-0-9888279-8-1; 68 pgs.; $15.95.

Kerry Shawn Keys
The Burning Mirror*
ISBN: 978-0-9772524-9-7; 92 pgs.; $14.95.
Book Of Beasts*
ISBN: 978-0-9800081-4-2; 64 pgs.; $12.95.
Transporting, A Cloak Of Rhapsodies*
ISBN: 978-0-9800081-8-0; 112 pgs.; $15.95.
Night Flight*
ISBN: 978-0-9831251-3-6; 96 pgs.; $15.95.

Arthur Winfield Knight
High Country
Chapbook; 32 pgs.; $6.00.
Champagne Dawns
Chapbook; 28 pgs.; $6.00.

Richard Kostelanetz
PO/EMS
Chapbook; 40 pgs.; $6.00.
More Fulcra Poems
Chapbook; 52 pgs.; $6.00.
Purling Sonnets
Chapbook; 32 pgs.; $6.00.

Linda Lerner
Living In Dangerous Times
Chapbook; 56 pgs.; $6.00.

Donald Lev

Only Wings - 20 Poems Of Devotion
Chapbook; 28 pgs.; $6.00.
Where I Sit
ISBN: 978-0-9888279-9-8; 88 pgs.; $15.95.

Lyn Lifshin
In Mirrors
ISBN: 978-0-9772524-3-5; 84 pgs.; $15.00.
Lost Horses
Chapbook; 36 pgs.; $6.00.

Gerald Locklin
From A Male Perspective
Chapbook; 32 pgs.; $6.00.
Deep Meanings - Selected Poems 2008-2013
ISBN: 978-0-9831251-9-8; 132 pg.; $16.95.

Peter Ludwin
Rumors Of Fallible Gods
ISBN: 978-0-9831251-8-1; 108 pgs.; $15.95.

Glenna Luschei
Seedpods
Chapbook; 40 pgs.; $6.00.
Total Immersion
ISBN: 978-0-9800081-0-4; 96 pgs.; $15.00.
Witch Dance - New & Selected Poems
ISBN: 978-0-9800081-7-3; 84 pgs.; $13.95.
Sprouts
Chapbook; 28 pgs.; $6.00.
Leaving It All Behind
ISBN: 978-0-9831251-2-9; 104 pgs.; $15.95.

Gary Metras
The Moon In The Pool
ISBN: 978-0-9888279-7-4; 68 pgs.; $12.95.
White Storm
ISBN: 978-0-9888279-9-6; 88 pgs.; $15.95.

Stanley Nelson
Pre-Socratic Points & Other New Poems*
ISBN: 978-0-9772524-4-2, 84 pgs.; $15.00.
Limbos For Amplified Harpsichord*
ISBN: 978-0-9772524-8-0; 144 pgs.; $17.95.
City Of The Sun*
ISBN: 978-0-9800081-2-8; 126 pgs.; $15.95.

B. Z. Niditch
Captive Cities

Chapbook; 36 pgs.; $8.00.

Roseanne Ritzema, Ed.
Inside The Outside - An Anthology Of Avant- Garde American Poets*
ISBN: 978-0-9772524-1-8; 304 pgs.; $29.95.
Poetry Matters - A Collection of Essays
ISBN: 978-0-9965026-3-4; 110 pgs.; $13.95.

Lynne Savitt
The Deployment Of Love In Pineapple Twilight
Chapbook; 48 pgs.; $6.00.

Steven Sher
Grazing On Stars - Selected Poems
ISBN: 978-0-9831251-7-4; 84 pgs.; $15.95.

Harry Smith
Up North (w/ Eric Greinke)
Chapbook; 40 pgs.; $6.00.
Little Things*
ISBN: 978-0-9800081-3-5; 78 pgs.; $13.95.

t. kilgore splake
Ghost Dancer's Dreams*
ISBN: 978-0-9831251-4-3; 68 pgs.; $12.95.
Coming Home
Chapbook; 36 pgs.; $6.00.
Splake Fishing In America*
ISBN: 978-0-9888279-1-2; 140 pgs.; $20.00.
Beyond The Ghosts
Chapbook; 36 pgs.; $6.00.
Winter River Flowing - Selected Poems 1979-2014
ISBN: 978-0-9888279-6-7; 152 pgs.; $21.95.
Tommy's Desk
ISBN: 978-0-9965026-2-7; 64 pages; $13.95.

Alison Stone
Dangerous Enough
ISBN: 978-0-9888279-3-6; 80 pgs.; $15.95.

Lloyd Van Brunt
Delirium - Selected Poems
Chapbook; 48 pgs.; $6.00.

Marine Robert Warden
Beyond The Straits*
ISBN: 978-0-980001-6-6; 72 pgs.; $13.95.

Leslie H. Whitten Jr.
The Rebel - Poems By Charles Baudelaire

Chapbook; 48 pgs.; $7.00.

A. D. Winans

The Other Side Of Broadway - Selected Poems
ISBN: 978-0-9772524-5-9; 132 pgs.; $18.00.
Wind On His Wings
Chapbook; 44 pgs.; $8.00.
This Land Is Not My Land
ISBN: 978-0-9888279-4-3; 60 pgs.; $14.95.

* currently out of print

Available through Baker & Taylor, The Book House,
Coutts Information Services, Midwest Library Services,local bookstores
& directly from the publisher - www.presapress.com.

Exclusive European Distribution through
Gazelle Book Service Ltd. - sales@gazellebooksco.uk

Also available as E-Books on Amazon.com

For The Living Dead – New & Selected Poems
(Eric Greinke)

Dangerous Enough
(Alison Stone)

This Land Is Not My Land
(A. D. Winans)

Where I Sit
(Donald Lev)

The Potential of Poetry
(Eric Greinke)

winter river flowing: selected poems 1979-2014
(t.kilgore splake)

Remarks and Reflections - Essays
(Kirby Congdon)

The Moon in the Pool
(Gary Metras)

retrievals
(Ruth Moon Kempher)

Zen Duende - Collaborative Poems
(Eric Greinke & Glenna Luschei)